D1312633

DISCARD
Wakarusa Public Library

Mastering
Martial Arts

A Complete Guide to

KARATE

STEFANO DI MARINO
ROBERTO GHETTI

Enslow Publishing
101 W. 23rd Street
Suite 240
New York, NY 10011
USA

enslow.com

Published in 2018 by Enslow Publishing, LLC.
101 W. 23rd Street, Suite 240, New York, NY 10011

© 2018 by Enslow Publishing, LLC.
© 2018 by DVE Publishing, worldwide, branch of Confidential Concepts, USA

All rights reserved.
No part of this book may be reproduced by any means without the written permission of
the publisher.

Library of Congress Cataloging-in-Publication Data
Names: Di Marino, Stefano, 1961- author. | Ghetti, Roberto, author.
Title: A complete guide to karate / Stefano Di Marino, Roberto Ghetti.
Description: New York, NY : Enslow Publishing, 2018. | Series: Mastering Martial Arts | Includes
bibliographical references and index. | Audience: Grade 9-12.
Identifiers: LCCN 2017001878 | ISBN 9780766085398 (library bound : alk. paper)
Subjects: LCSH: Karate—Juvenile literature.
Classification: LCC GV1114.3 D573 2018 | DDC 796.815/3—dc23
LC record available at https://lccn.loc.gov/2017001878

Printed in the United States of America

To Our Readers: We have done our best to make sure all websites in this book were active and
appropriate when we went to press. However, the author and the publisher have no control over
and assume no liability for the material available on those websites or on any websites they may
link to. Any comments or suggestions can be sent by e-mail to customerservice@enslow.com.

Photo Credits: Cover © Lucian Coman | Shutterstock

All interior images © by DVE Publishing, worldwide, branch of Confidential Concepts, USA.

Contents

Introduction

A long with judo, karate is a martial art that, for various reasons, has experienced enormous popularity with athletes and fans for the past thirty years. Japanese organizations have managed to disseminate a uniform image of karate and *karatekas* (students) across a varying range of karate styles. Karate presents a well-structured, easily recognizable discipline for the general public, and it is easily distinguishable from Chinese, Vietnamese, and Thai combat styles.

Japan's effective and consistent influence of martial arts styles in the West has been widespread: Enoeda in England, Kase in France, and Shirai in Italy are some examples of the proliferation of Japanese martial arts. Following this mass diffusion, karate teachers have since created a meticulous technical preparation

The symbol for karate.

done with a willingness to spread a rigorous and universally accessible combat style; these are just some of the reasons for karate's longevity and continued success. As it stands today, karate is a discipline that, for those who commit enthusiastically, can offer psychophysical education, as well as an opportunity to participate in a competitive sport.

We are opposed to an excessively specialized idea of karate, a vision desired by certain organizations that exclusively develop profiles based on different styles. The karate we practice and love is a complex discipline in which formal exercises and combat techniques merge. While karate's applications in competition and self-defense are important, they are not its only uses.

To excel in the practice and study of karate, we of course recommend that you take a class at a specialized gym taught by skilled, trained professionals. With this spirit, but fully accepting the necessity of having a teacher, we offer this illustrated guide to karate. Our objective is to provide an elaborate introduction to the discipline's fundamental techniques, regardless of the variety of styles presented in most gyms today.

We analyze fundamental positions and techniques and propose a basic selection of attacks and counterattacks. Readers who are familiar with the basic attacks and responses will find the sections on more complex techniques useful and enlightening. We close the volume with two *kata*, or formal exercises, that students should practice alone: confronting themselves and fighting against their own shadow. These are two basic exercises (*kata heian shodan* and *kata pinan shodan*) that students learn in the first few months, in the *shotokan* style (one of the most practiced) and the *shitoryu* style, respectively. In the differences and variations of these basic techniques, the reader will find interesting information for personal growth, as well as guidance on improving within the discipline.

How to Use This Book

We suggest you read the book first, without attempting to remember any combinations or trying to master every strike listed at the beginning of the lessons. When you have an idea of the technical arsenal of karate and its fundamental principles, study each chapter until you learn how to confidently perform different strikes and learn different moves.

You'll then be able to practice with a partner, first in the simplest forms of closed combat and then in a more open form. Once you have enough experience to practice with a partner and comfortably use techniques like blocks, you will be able to study more complex combinations.

When your abilities have improved, you can venture into new forms of training, like the ones in the chapter dedicated to combat. You will perform combinations that are formal but open, and which are specific to whoever chooses them at the moment of attack or block.

We will finally arrive at *kumite* (open combat), which should always be performed with controlled strikes. Here you will learn that the kumite is an exercise in which the karatekas face each other, respecting each other's integrity, with the objective to perform correctly and not beat an opponent violently or without coordination.

Following tradition, all of the techniques and parts of the body are described in Japanese with their translation in parentheses. The translations cannot, of course, be literal, as they would be rendered meaningless. The photographic sequences of techniques are accompanied with descriptions.

The History and Spread of Karate

Okinawa and the Martial Tradition of the Ryukyu Islands

Okinawa is the most important of the small chain of islands situated exactly between Japan and China in the South China Sea. The fishers and navigators of the Ryukyu Islands have always held an important position in the contact between the Empire of the Rising Sun and the Kingdom of Midday. Traders and sailors traveled carrying goods and naturally shared martial techniques. The necessity to defend the island against the Wako Japanese pirates, and the inevitable contact between guards and warriors, influenced the evolution of combat techniques in Okinawa and the rest of the Ryukyu Islands.

We have evidence of war practice—although not strictly martial—in Okinawa dating from the seventeenth century. From what we know, the combat methods were crude, almost prehistoric. The martial evolution of Okinawa essentially followed two routes that, in light of their geographical situation, seem predictable today.

On one side, we see a clear influence of the Chinese school of combat, which Okinawan mariners picked up in ports like Fukien (where Okinawan settlements had existed since ancient times). On the other hand, their

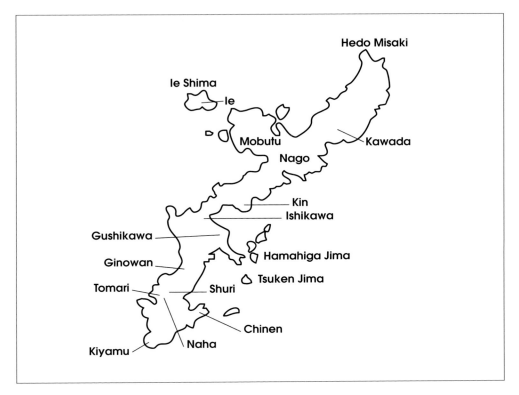

The island of Okinawa.

aggressive Japanese neighbors arrived on the archipelago bringing their own martial arts.

At the turn of the tenth century and after their defeat against the Minamoto clan, the Taira clan searched for refuge on the beaches of Okinawa. They introduced weapons and martial ceremonies that were quickly adopted by the governing elite of the archipelago. Divided into principalities by standing combatants, the inhabitants of Okinawa achieved unity in the thirteenth century under the Shunten dynasty, a regime rigidly marked by Japanese models.

In this same period, the development of Okinawan martial arts increased decisively with techniques inspired by the Japanese *budo* (path of combat), just as China influenced local arts at this time. It is noteworthy that at this point, the Okinawan sovereigns had already banned the use of sharp weapons in towns, a decision sometimes erroneously attributed to the successive Japanese invasions in the seventeenth century.

The Okinawan martial development can be thusly summed up: the nobility fundamentally practiced a form of Japanese-inspired budo that favored the use of weapons. The towns, on the other hand, preferred systems of government rooted in Chinese tradition, some of which allowed the use of arms, while others did not. The dissemination of the latter had great success and eventually spread among the nobility.

Tang Hand

Contrary to the combat style that came from Japan, where body-to-body fighting methods gave priority to the defender (the one attacked) and thrusts were used to take down an opponent (a result of the use of armor, which rendered strikes useless and forced fighters to develop techniques that served them from a grounded position or helped them disarm a soldier), in Okinawa, disarmed combat developed for the most part between private opponents as a form of protection.

A modern karate combat.

A spectacular kick during a karate exhibition.

The influence of the Chinese school and its divisions between "hard" and "soft" styles found its correspondence in the combat schools of Okinawa. These developed along a geographic distribution in relation to the different cities. Each city followed its own style from a region in China and enjoyed mutual commercial and cultural contacts with the Kingdom of Midday.

The techniques practiced in the city of Shuri, for example, are strongly inspired by the "hard" styles of Chinese boxing, derived from the school of the Shaolin Temple. This was a style that gave priority to quick movements, sometimes of remarkable force, and was always based on an application of power. Conversely, in Naha, a technique influenced by internal or "soft" styles was practiced originally in the Wudang region of northern China, where the modern version of tai chi originated.

Due to the Okinawans' pragmatic spirit, and mixed with necessity, they adapted sophisticated Taoist elaborations of internal Chinese styles, both fluid and refined, to use the *chi*'s internal energy. The use of chi created an easier technique and contrasted with the "hard" style inspired by circular movements.

Conversely, in Tomari, people practiced a style that unified the characteristics of their school into a fusion between "hard" and "soft," which was the base of the Goju school (meaning literally "hard and soft"), the style most characteristic of Okinawan karate.

The school maintained an indisputably Chinese influence,

Gichin Funakoshi, founder of the Shotokan style.

so much that the transcription of the name, *Tode*, reflected its Chinese origins so strongly that the Japanese found it unbearable. *Te* meant "hand" and alluded to the use of the human body as a weapon. The term *to* can be translated as "empty" (in the sense of "uncovered hands") but was also like *tang*, a written character that in this era was associated with China.

The Tode, the martial art of Okinawa, was thus the technique of the uncovered hand, but also of the "Tang hand"—the Chinese school of martial arts.

During this period, other events matured the social and martial practices of the Ryukyu Islands. In 1600, Tokugawa Ieyasu was elevated to the title of shogun in Japan (the military governor appointed by the emperor). In order to bring the Honshu Island clan—a distrustful and powerful group—under the control of the Satsuma, the shogun offered the clan's leader the opportunity to seize and take over the neighboring islands of Ryukyu. Since then, Ryukyu has formed a stable, though not official, part of the Japanese empire.

The impact of the invaders was difficult on the lives of the archipelago's inhabitants. Stripping authority from the local nobility, the samurai of Satsuma imposed fees and a regime we can only imagine was poorly supported by the population. Naturally, the Satsuma prohibited the practice of all martial arts and the Tode; revealing Chinese origins was only done in secret.

Despite the beliefs of some romantics, we don't have concrete evidence about how the bare-handed or primitively armed inhabitants of Okinawa confronted the shielded samurais, who were heavily armed with swords and spears. After all, the Tode and the existing defense techniques were not systems of magical combat, and a samurai armed with a sword was, in reality, an invincible war machine.

However, it is necessary to recognize that in a period of such war and banditry, many people found occasions to use martial arts as self-defense.

Following the Meiji Restoration in 1868, the samurai class disappeared, and a ban on sword carrying was enforced on professionals. During this time, Japan faced radical combat in which Okinawan influence and martial techniques took center stage.

Why the surge of Okinawan influence? First of all, the Ryukyu Islands had been a stable part of Japan for some time. Secondly, many restrictions were made on the population, and with them came an anger that motivated the inhabitants to practice martial arts.

The Okinawan inhabitants' passion for unarmed combat had not weakened, and when the ban on its practice was lifted, local martial arts once again began to develop in the light of day. In fact, martial arts flourished so much that in 1903 the Tode was included in the archipelago's school curriculum (definitive proof that it wasn't truly prohibited).

During this same period, Japanese martial arts changed radically, passing from *jitsu* (the art of military application) to *do* (the belief that an improved existence is attained through fighting exercises). Jigoro Kano developed a system of codification for the acquisition of judo, and this organization was also used in Okinawan combat arts: Gichin Funakoshi, a professor from the expert school of Tode, was invited by Kano to Tokyo to demonstrate his art for the Japanese emperor.

The Japanese passion for this new combat style was immediate and sweeping. Soon, the Okinawan fighting technique was imported and incorporated into the budo discipline, adopted in schools and universities.

Naturally, the problem of the name still remained; in the early twentieth century, Japan experienced a wave of renewed imperialism, and the Chinese connotation (Tang hand) was deemed unacceptable. Therefore, a compromise was made, but not without a certain reluctance by the most severe Okinawan masters: the new martial art, in the modern codified version of Funakoshi, would be called karate. *Kara* was a word that meant "empty" within the meaning of "bare hand" and, at the same time, alluded to the concept of an "empty mind," a Zen idea indicating a mind free from obstacles and directed solely toward one's objective. Thus, it was born as karate-do, a martial art that, although of Chinese origin, had acquired definitive Japanese characteristics.

Karate in the World

Since its spread in Japan in the 1920's, karate has fragmented into a myriad of schools, sometimes giving dedicated teachers the possibility of expressing their personal combat vision and sometimes for sports policy reasons. The technical validity of the new discipline is accepted across the board due to its spread throughout the world. In reality, only fragments of the sometimes brutal combat art of Okinawa have remained, and the karate practiced today has an especially sporty, educational purpose. It's equally true that the technical arsenal of karate has expanded enormously (for example, the roundhouse kick—the *mawashi geri*—is a recent introduction), and throughout the world karate has become synonymous with "punch and kick" martial arts par excellence. Perhaps karate will never make it to the Olympic Games (surpassed by tae kwon do, which is represented as an organized discipline in a unique style under only two international federations), but the extent of its dissemination and the accessibility of its techniques for young students and those less gifted with athletic abilities has made it popular today. It is ultimately a discipline that, regardless of fads, continues to consistently grow its number of students.

The Objective of This Book

Shotokan, Shitoryu, *Wadoryu, Kyokushinkai*…a beginner can get lost in the many styles making up karate today. We do not have space to delve into every school, and furthermore, our intention here is to create a broad text accessible to all.

We will therefore limit ourselves to an introduction of the basic techniques, positions, moves, and common strategies used in all styles of karate.

We intend to outline a technical base so that you can practice and improve your abilities if you're already a student of any style, or so that you can familiarize yourself with the possibilities offered by all schools of combat derived from the Tode of Okinawa. Of course, it should be remembered that the direction of a teacher is always necessary.

Karate Styles

Apart from being a unitary discipline based in the same "grammar" (punching, kicking, striking, and blocking techniques), today karate is divided into "styles," or schools, that practice combat with slightly different qualities.

Recent decades have seen a true proliferation of styles, originating especially from every teacher's desire to be remembered as a founder of a particular method. Below, we offer a short description of the major styles of karate, avoiding the purely commercial schools and schools of minor importance.

Shotokan: Founded by Gichin Funakoshi, Shotokan is the first style of Japanese karate-do derived from the *Shuri-te* and *Naha-te* schools of Okinawa.

Gojuryu: Founded by Chojun Miyagi, Gojuryu is the modern fighting style from Okinawa; it has also developed a Japanese branch headed by the well-known (and now deceased) Yamaguchi Gogen, dubbed "the cat" for his agility.

Wadoryu: Founded by Hirinori Otsuka, a teacher of Japanese ju jitsu who united the typical Okinawan striking techniques of karate with the fight throws from his original school.

Shitoryu: Founded by Kenwa Mabuni in the 1930s, this style originated in Okinawa and was codified in Japan. Given that Mabuni knew the *shuri* style like the *tomari* and *naha*, they were elaborated afterward according to Mabuni's personal criteria.

Shokukai: Founded by Chojiro Tani, *shokukai* was derived from Shitoryu.

Sankukai: Founded by Yoshinao Nanbu, who originally practiced *shokukai* and aikido. Nanbu later reworked his style and created the *nanbudo*, a psychophysical educational system in which the martial aspect, particularly the development of internal energy, played a less prominent role.

Shorinji Kempo: Founded by the master Doshin So, a Buddhist monk who, during World War II, acted as a Japanese secret agent in China to learn martial secrets. In effect, *shorinji* is the Japanese transcription of "shaolin," and Shorinji is inspired more by Chinese combat styles than Okinawan. His teachings possess a strong philosophical component.

Kyokushinkai: Founded by the master Masutatu Oyama, kyokushinkai is the most singular of all karate styles. For example, combat includes real contact and allows kicks to the legs. Based especially in physical preparation, it is more similar to kickboxing (performed without gloves) than to proper karate. It is one of the fastest-growing styles in terms of the Japanese public's preference, and in just a few years, it has generated a myriad of substyles.

Λ Karate Lesson

We begin our journey into the world of karate by introducing ourselves to the rituals between master and student. We will then see the structure of karate teachings and the execution of more complex techniques.

Places, Divisions, Levels, and Training

Karate is practiced and studied in a *dojo*. The student dresses in a *kimono* (karate suit) complete with an *obi* (belt) of different colors according to the *kyu* (grade) to which the student belongs. The kimono is white, and the *kyugo* range from level 6 to level 1. The *dan* levels (degrees of belt) go in increasing order:

6. White belt

5. Yellow belt

4. Orange belt

3. Green belt

2. Blue belt

1. Purple belt

The training can last from an hour to an hour and a half twice a week. Students preparing for competition will train more frequently, and sessions will usually last anywhere from an hour and a half to two hours.

CATEGORIES OF AGE AND WEIGHT

Age Category	Male Weight Categories	Female Weight Categories
Cadets (Ages 14-15)	115 lbs. (152 kg.), 115-126 lbs. (52-57 kg) 126-139 lbs. (57-63 kg) 139-155 lbs. (63-70 kg) 155+ lbs. (70+ kg.)	104 lbs. (47 kg) 104-120 lbs. (47-54 kg) 120+ lbs. (54+ kg)
Juniors (Ages 16-17)	122 lbs. (55 kg.) 122-135 lbs. (55-61 kg) 135-150 lbs. (61-68 kg) 150-168 lbs. (68-76 kg) 168+ lbs. (76+ kg)	106 lbs. (48 kg) 106-117 lbs. (48-53 kg) 117-131 lbs. (53-59 kg) 131+ lbs. (59+ kg)
Under 21 (Ages 18-20)	133 lbs. (60 kg) 133-148 lbs. (60-67 kg) 148-166 lbs. (67-75 kg) 166-186 lbs. (75-84 kg) 186+ lbs. (84+ kg)	111 lbs. (50 kg) 111-122 lbs. (50-55 kg) 122-135 lbs. (55-61 kg) 135-150 lbs. (61-68 kg) 150+ lbs. (68+ kg)
Seniors (Ages 16 and over for kata) (Ages 18 and over for kumite)	133 lbs. (60 kg) 133-148 lbs. (60-67 kg) 148-166 lbs. (67-75 kg) 166-186 lbs. (75-84 kg) 186+ lbs. (84+ kg)	111 lbs. (50 kg) 111-122 lbs. (50-55 kg) 122-135 lbs. (55-61 kg) 135-150 lbs. (61-68 kg) 150+ lbs. (68+ kg)
Noncompetitors (Ages 13 and over)	No weight restrictions apply to students who do not want to or cannot train for competition, or who have surpassed the indicated age limit for competition.	

The Greeting

As in all martial arts, the greeting is fundamentally important in karate. It is not just a simple formality; the greeting is an act of courtesy that shows respect from the student in combat to the student's partners.

There are two forms of greeting used in karate. The first and most common is *ritsurei* (standing greeting), which is usually used in exercises or before the execution of the kata (form or model).

The karatekas (karate students) stand opposite each other and bow at a 45° angle or lower.

The other form of greeting is *zarei* (kneeling greeting), which the teacher and the student typically perform at the beginning or end of each lesson.

Taiso

The *taiso* begins after the ritual greeting at the start of the lesson as a warm-up. It's a very important part of the karate lesson, although it's not a proper part of the technique.

The warm up and physical preparation are fundamental in every discipline; it's important to emphasize this now, especially for those who are trying karate for the first time and for those starting to train after a period of inactivity. Periodic training, and especially

consistent training, will help improve two aspects:

- The physical form, which helps the student perform exercises more often and without suffering injuries or resistance problems due to physical force
- The correct execution of the movements without the fear of hurting oneself due to lack of physical preparation

As you can see, these two things are closely connected. If students pay consistent and correct attention to physical training, they will improve and enhance their technical abilities.

Every professor has his own system, and each creates a series of open exercises that generally take up the first ten to fifteen minutes of class. These exercises are designed to gradually activate, tone, and boost the body before it is open to movements that, if done without a warm up, carry the risk of bone fractures and other injuries.

Naturally, when beginning any new physical activity, it is wise to increase the intensity of the exercise gradually in order to prevent injury.

To produce a noticeable improvement and maintain good physical condition, a student should attend at least two training sessions per week. After every training session, the student will likely notice an improvement in her movements, muscular capacity, coordination, and stamina. Consistent training can lead to a physical improvement of the body. A fit physical form includes good muscle tone, which is especially important in karate. In fact, a state of continuous muscular tension, intermittent with a state of rest, facilitates physiological functions like good posture and increased blood flow to the heart.

From a strictly athletic point of view, a suitable muscle tone allows for an immediate and effective muscle contraction response, essential for technical improvement. Finally, on an aesthetic level, a good muscle tone leads to a state of well-being, which can be improved even further with periodic training of the body.

A general athletic preparation often includes all types of training to achieve a better muscular condition.

The following proposed exercises seek to improve a karate student's muscular power, coordination, and joint mobility.

Increasing your internal body temperature, similar to warming up a car, allows you to perform at your highest capacity. Once you achieve optimal physical condition, you have many advantages:

- Better blood flow to the muscles, thanks to vasodilatation and an increased heart rate
- A more rapid and efficient transfer of hemoglobin oxygen
- An increase and improvement of metabolic change and use of various energies
- Ease of nerve impulse transmissions and elevation of the sensitivity threshold for neuromuscular receptors
- Reduction of muscle viscosity, with the possibility of more rapid and powerful contractions

- Improvement of the elastic properties of muscles, tendons, and cartilage, with the consequent elevation of the mechanical function and preventative action of any eventual injuries that can occur

The diverse forms of execution, complexity, speed, and time of execution can be used to improve important factors like coordination, speed, strength, and general resistance. Exercise examples (in progression):

1. Walk at a quick pace.
2. Run in a gentle rhythm.
3. Run sideways.
4. Run in various styles.

Here are some examples of static warm-up exercises:

1. Jump and rotate your neck (twisting or bending the neck side to side and up and down).
2. Bend your torso forward and sideways.
3. Rotate your core (without excessive bowing backward).
4. Sit on the floor, widen your legs, and while maintaining openness, bend your chest and core forward.

5. After closing your legs, bend forward again and, without bending your knees, try to touch your face to your knees.

6. Bring your feet together, coupling them in front of your pelvis. With your forearms bent above the legs, try to reach your face to your feet.

7. Exercise your abdominals.

8. Bend your knees and elbows.

This warm-up phase concludes with stretches and appropriate exercises suitable for karate, which we'll detail later.

Obviously you can't invent an optimal, personalized diet yourself; any change in diet should be advised by a doctor, dietician, or sports specialist whose knowledge can be very useful.

After warming up, we can start training, attentively studying the basic techniques of karate. Generally, the exercises can be done alone or with a partner.

Tobacco and alcohol are harmful and noxious, and they limit the ability to improve and enjoy the benefits of athletics; reduce, or better yet, eliminate these bad habits.

For the partnered exercises, the two karatekas traditionally adopt the role of *kogeki* (offensive karateka), most commonly *tori* (the one who initiates), and *uke* (the one who defends and counterattacks). As we have mentioned, the ritsurei should be performed at the beginning and end of each activity.

The Basic Techniques of Karate

Karate is among the martial arts in which striking techniques are greatly used. In the majority of cases, karatekas will use strikes defensively to dominate their opponent, using them only occasionally (or more properly as throws) and always continuing with a decisive strike technique, the *ate waza*.

Karate's technical arsenal can be divided into four groups. We will examine these later, so readers can have an idea of what techniques they have at their disposal:

- *tsuki* (punch technique)
- *keri* (kick technique)
- *uchi* (strike technique)
- *uke* (block technique)

Tsuki

Tsuki, or punches, make up a large part of the karateka's technical arsenal. Contrary to many Chinese styles derived from kung fu, karate frequently utilizes the fists.

In ancient times, the fists were reinforced with ointments and special training, in which the student repeatedly hit a *makiwara* (a hard surface made of woven straw) to strengthen the hand. Fundamentally, the tsuki is used in a direct line, but circular strikes also exist, delivered with an upward trajectory (similar to the uppercut in boxing).

Keri

Keri, or kicks, are without a doubt the most spectacular techniques. Exhibitions and movies have shown impressive possibilities of kicking (jumping strikes to the face). In the original version of karate, which was oriented toward self-defense, keri were almost always inflicted to the waist or below; this gives the opponent fewer possibilities to support himself and makes it easier to push him down.

Uchi

Uchi, or literally percussions, are strikes that don't properly fit into the tsuki category, despite the fact that they're usually directed at upper joints.

Strikes thrown with the back of the hand, the side of the hand, and the elbow are considered uchi. Front and circular knee strikes are also included in this group, which in karate are used for self-defense at a short distance.

Uke

The blocks make up the framework for karate defense. Principally based on low positions and movements at a large distance, modern karate uses, in a limited way, these elusive techniques typically seen in Western boxing. In karate, the main instrument of defense is uke, the block used to intercept the opponent's attack, which diverts the trajectory.

A block made with energy and appropriate speed can reveal itself to be an effective counterattack, given that it produces a hit above the attacker's joint and impedes subsequent attack attempts.

To correctly perform these techniques, it's necessary to maintain a low center of gravity with your legs slightly bent and aligned with your shoulders, which should be level throughout all positions.

Performance of oi tsuki, attack with forward fist.

The spirit of karate lives in the block: it demonstrates the fact that all formal exercises (the kata) begin with the block, to teach students to initiate an act of offense only after they have been assaulted.

Controlling the Strikes

In modern karate, which is understood as an educational and sports-based discipline, the concept of the controlled strike is fundamental. During all exercises, two students perform attacks and blocks with the spirit of cooperation, "diverting" the technique a few centimeters from the objective (sometimes millimeters if the athlete is an expert) to prevent hurting the training partner.

The concept of control is fundamental in karate-do, where the base principle is the student's improvement through the study of a fighting technique.

Karate Weapons

The karate "weapons" are the parts of the body used in attack and defense. In karate, it is possible to strike with every part of the body, although the recent sports-based evolution has led to a lack of technical expertise. It's necessary to remember that before karate was seen as a method of self-defense, it was based mainly on the idea of using the human body as a weapon.

How to Hit with a Fist

In karate protective gloves are used only in open combat, which we will talk about later. For now, it's important to learn how to close the fist correctly to avoid injuries in training, like dislocations, sprains, and sometimes even fractured fingers.

1. Extend your hand and fold the first part of the fingers, closing the fingers over the palm.

2. Close the thumb over the fingers, remembering that the fist should be perfectly aligned with the wrist.

3. Throw the strike only with the knuckles of the index and middle finger (in the zone called *seiken*). You do this for two reasons: first, because when throwing a punch, the full force of the body accumulates in the middle finger (which extends out the farthest); second, because the smaller the surface where the force is centered, the greater the effect and penetration of the strike.

The zones of impact are identified with a continuous line.

OTHER FORMS OF STRIKING

There are many ways of striking an opponent. For example, a student can throw by using *shuto* (which uses the outside of the hand), *koshi* (using the sole of the foot), and *sokuto* (using the outer part of the foot).

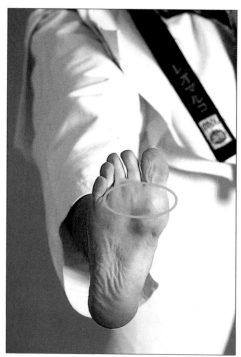

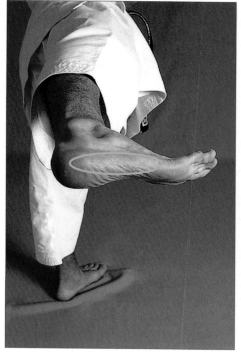

Positions and Moves

I n karate the word *dachi* is used to refer to the position. The denomination of the positions is always based on a double term, in which the description of the posture of the feet is combined with the suffix "dachi"; for example "*teiji dachi*," or natural position in a T.

In the study of combat, and karate in particular, the correct execution of attack and defense techniques depends largely on the position of the lower joints; before starting the study of the techniques, students should familiarize themselves with the basic positions and moves.

Every martial art presents many different basic positions. In the following pages, all the techniques are explained, whether offensive or defense. Learning the positions well and studying balance and different possibilities is one of our first exercises. Only after you've mastered balance can you learn how to perform the different techniques combined with foot positions and movements.

HEISOKU DACHI (Natural Position)

This is an upright position in which the body is relaxed, feet together, legs slightly bent, arms at one's sides, hands on top of the thighs, and fingers together. It is one of the first positions learned because many exercises start from this position.

MUSUBI DACHI (Natural Position with Feet Apart)

We have already discussed the two kinds of greetings: one on foot and the other kneeling. This is the position that, before and after each partnered technical exercise, or at the beginning and end of the kata, is adopted to perform the foot greeting (remember that the zarei is only performed at the beginning and end of each lesson).

This is an upright, relaxed posture with heels together and feet pointing away from each other. The hands are held at one's sides with the fingers together.

HACHIJI DACHI (Natural Position with Legs Apart)

Upright position with the legs separated; the feet are placed at the same width as the shoulders. This is done before basic techniques or to begin a kata. The arms are kept by the sides of the body, and the body is relaxed.

HEIKO DACHI (Natural Position with Feet Parallel)

This position is similar to the previous one, but the feet are parallel to each other. The hands are closed into fists.

TEIJI DACHI (Natural Position with Feet in a T)

The feet form a kind of straight T, with the back foot (the horizontal part of the T) positioned straight and inward. The heel of the front foot should be separated from the instep of the back foot by about twelve inches (about 30.5 centimeters).

RENOJI DACHI (Position with Feet in an L)

The feet form an L: an imaginary line cuts the front foot longitudinally and, the heel perpendicularly brushes against the heel of the back foot.

ZENKUTSU DACHI (Forward Frontal Position)

From the *hachiji dachi* position, the body is kept upright and perpendicular to the ground. The right foot stays immobile. The left is placed close by, so that it completely displaces the weight of the body onto the right leg, which should be slightly bent. The right leg should push the sole of the foot down to completely support the body, and the sole of the right foot forces the left foot forward to create a space almost double that of the hachiji dachi.

The front leg is bent and the knee stays perpendicular over the instep of the foot, while the back leg stays extended. The shoulders are on the same horizontal plane; the back foot should be exactly 45° from the front foot.

THE MOVEMENTS

The intermediate phases of the *zenkutsu dachi* positions are also some of the most common forms used in karate to advance and retreat.

To correctly perform the displacements, you should remember a few rules:

- Keep the body perpendicular to the ground.
- Keep the height constant while moving, without swaying.
- The back leg should stay bent when advancing.
- The sole of the foot of the back leg (which pushes) should be completely supported on the ground.

ADVANCE AND RETREAT

Try to advance with your hands by your sides and afterward return to the starting position; repeat the same movement until you have no difficulty and the action is harmonious and automatic.

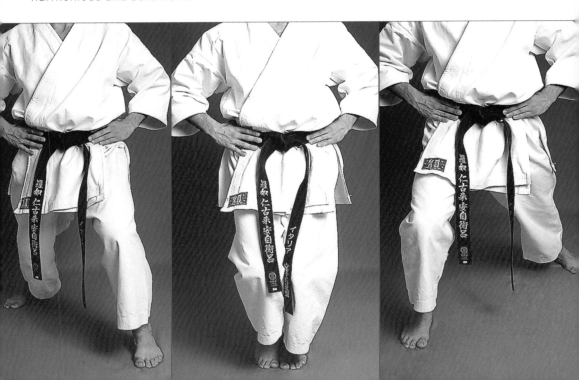

CHANGING DIRECTION

1. When your training area is limited and it's not possible to go any further, you should turn to continue the exercise. The most efficient way to change directions is by turning and returning to the zenkutsu dachi position. Remember that the foot of your front leg stays fixed.

2. Move your back leg twenty-four inches (about 61 centimeters) around toward the back.

3.   Raising the heel of your back leg, rotate the hips over the front part of your front leg: you will be in the same position but facing the other way (in the photo sequence the *gedan barai* technique is performed with the arms; see page 68). Now you can start the exercise again. In the dojo, it is the professor who, during practice, gives the order to rotate with the word *mawatte* (turn).

KOKUTSU DACHI (Position on Back Leg)

Place yourself in the teiji dachi position and advance with your left leg. The right should not move; keep the weight of your body a bit more on the back leg than the front.

KIBA DACHI (Rider Position)

This is a symmetrical position that offers good stability. While it is used frequently in the kata, it is not used much in sporting combat. The feet are parallel to each other, and the weight of the body is distributed evenly above both legs. The knees simultaneously "push" outward; the body is upright, and the glutes are flexed.

SHIKO DACHI (Square Position)

This position is similar to the previous one but with the feet open at a 45° angle and the knees bent slightly lower.

FUDO DACHI
(Consolidated Position)

This is a combination of zenkutsu dachi and *kiba dachi*, which changes the direction of the feet; it's a strong position intended to immediately block and counterattack. The knees should be bent and at the same time angled and pushed outward. Distribute the weight equally between the feet.

NEKO ASHI DACHI
(Cat Position)

For this position, begin with *kokutsu dachi* and move the foot forward until the heel cannot rise any higher and only the front part of the foot lightly touches the ground; support most of your body with the back leg, which is slightly bent.

SANCHIN DACHI
(Hourglass Position)

Position both feet inward, with the knees slightly bent. Keep the core perpendicular to the ground and tighten the lower part of the abdomen, like in the previous positions. Important: support the foot at a distance similar to the width of the sides. Do not bend the knees too far inward, to avoid debilitating the outside and reducing stability.

HANGETSUDACHI (Half-Moon Position)

This position is somewhere between zenkutsu dachi, due to the placement of the feet (although there's only a small distance between them), and *sanchin dachi*, since the knees are forced inward.

KAMAE (Guard Position)

This is one of the positions used in the technical phase of karate; the body should be strong, stable, and balanced, and it should allow for fast movements in all direction without losing balance.

You should be in the position to confront both an attack phase and a defense phase, with the joints ready to strike or block as needed.

The *kamae* can be *hidari* (left), with the left leg forward, or *migi* (right), with the right leg forward, in a position similar to zenkutsu dachi.

Fundamental Techniques

The moment has arrived to study the *kihon*—the karate basic techniques. For practical reasons, we will group them here, to learn and perform them all together, but without rushing. Remember that in a traditional school, the student can spend months practicing a specific strike. Of course, it's not necessary to go to this extreme, but it's certainly true that in order to fully understand karate (as with other disciplines), it's preferable to learn by gradually moving up the levels of technical complexity only after a student has completely mastered the simpler moves.

In karate, the student learns to execute blocks and counterattacks alone, advancing and retreating in a straight line. Knowing that the discipline has numerous positions, in the kihon phase of study, the zenkutsu dachi position is most preferably used.

The master Hiroshi Shirai (right) during an action-packed exhibition.

Tsuki: Punching Techniques

First we will observe how to correctly use *tsuki* (the fist strikes aimed directly at our objective). Other techniques will follow from there.

CHOKU TSUKI (Back Punch)

To perform technical gestures correctly, place yourself in hachiji dachi. Move your fist from your side, rotating the forearm 180° and completely stretching your arm outward. The areas of attack are conventionally defined.

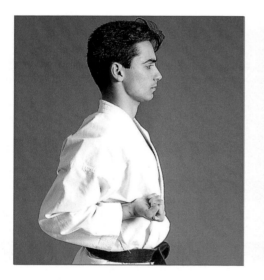

- *Jodan* (high, from the shoulders upward)
- *Chudan* (medium, from the core)
- *Gedan* (low, from the groin down)

OI TSUKI (Front Punch)

1. Begin the action in the hidari zenkutsu dachi gedan barai position.

2. Now take a large step forward with the right leg. The arms are firm, the fists closed.

3. Repositioning the left arm at your side, throw the right fist after taking a step.

The forward movement of the body gives force to the striking technique, allowing for a strong hit. Here the application of *hidari oi tsuki jodan* is shown in the final phase. Important: Don't lift your moving foot forward too much; slide it over the floor, moving it forward as quickly as possible.

GYAKU TSUKI (Opposite Punch)

1. Begin the action in the hidari zenkutsu dachi position. Extend the right arm forward and bend your left arm by your side. Position your left leg forward.

2. Take a large step forward with your right leg; your arms should be firm and your fists closed.

3. Return your right arm to your side and thrust out the left fist after taking a step and achieving a balanced, stable position.

Here the application of *chudan gyaku tsuki* is shown in the final phase. Remember: Do not lift the advancing foot too much—it's better to slide it over the floor and move it forward as quickly as possible. At the end of the movement, the weight of the body shouldn't be too far forward. The technique begins and ends with a side rotation, which stays at the same height throughout the movement; this movement transmits strength to the chest, the shoulders, the arms, and the fist.

MAWASHI TSUKI (Circular Punch Movement)

Starting from the hidari kamae, direct the fist from your side to the objective, striking with seiken; the thumb should be placed down at the moment of impact. The trajectory follows a circular movement toward the objective, which is often at the side of the face or the side of the core. Accompany the strike with a rotational movement from the corresponding side. This technique is reminiscent of the boxing hook and can be performed with both the front and back leg.

URA TSUKI (Inverted Punch)

This is performed from below upward, rotating the forearm in a way that the back of the fist turns downward at the moment of impact, which can be the face, the solar plexus, or with the sides. This technique is reminiscent of the uppercut in boxing and can be done by both the front and rear leg.

Keri: Kicking Techniques

MAE GERI (Front Kick)

1. From hidari kamae, lift your knee, keeping the sole of your foot and tibia perpendicular to the ground, with the front part of your foot a little more elevated than the heel (imagine you're stepping over a knee-high box).

2. Now stretch your leg and elevate your toes to strike the objective with koshi.

MAWASHI GERI (Roundhouse Kick)

1. From hidari kamae, lift your knee to the height of your abdomen with your foot at your side.

2. Straighten your leg with a circular movement and strike your objective with *haisoku* (the instep of the foot). For a better execution, completely bend your knee in a way that the heel almost touches your ribs and keeps the sole of your foot well supported on the ground.

YOKO GERI (Side Kick)

1. From hidari damae, elevate your knee in a form similar to *mae geri*. Rotate and stagger your body with your sides toward the objective so that you lift and bend your knee, brushing your foot against the inner part of the knee of the supporting leg.

2. When you stretch your leg and strike with sokuto, always place your toes forward and the outer edge of your foot down with the sole parallel to the floor.

YOKO GERI KEAGE (Jumping Kick); KEKOMI (Impulse Kick)

This is a swift kick with an immediate return of the foot to the starting position, almost in a semicircle. This has little strength at impact, and it is difficult to control balance; but at the same time, it eliminates the risk of being held by an opponent's leg. To perform *yoko geri kekomi* (impulse kick) with the intention of taking down the opponent, you must push, keeping the shortest and most direct trajectory possible, and focus the majority of the force of impact on the final phase.

FUMI KOMI (Swing Kick)

This kick is very effective against the knee or instep of the opponent's foot; it can be performed forward, backward, or to the side. It's particularly useful for freeing yourself from the opponent holding on to you. Push your foot back laterally and strike the objective with *kakato* (heel) or sokuto (edge of the foot), as if it were a sharp axe cutting the objective. Support all your weight on the striking leg while forcefully pushing down to strengthen the strike.

USHIRO GERI
(Rotating Kick)

1. Strike your heel toward your opponent, who is behind you. Beginning in the hidari kamae, lift the knee while observing your opponent.

2. Bring your heel backward and strike with kakato. Your foot should be at a 45° angle from the floor.

URA MAWASHI GERI (Inverted Circular Kick)

1. This kick is based on the principle of mawashi geri, but with an inverted circular leg movement.

2. Strike with koshi or kakato.

YOKO TOBI GERI (Jumping Side Kick)

This technique, which we will explain in the final phase of teaching, is truly spectacular and reserved for experts.

It is not used often in training lessons, or kata, but is used more for demonstrations; a valid execution of this or other flying kick techniques require a lot of training and notable athletic qualities. Considering the danger of execution, we advise the presence of a qualified teacher to ensure correct study and good training.

Ashi Barai (Foot Sweep)

This is a protective technique—it is used as a distraction or a feint during an attack or as an authentic opportunity to protect against your opponent and continue with a strike. It can be performed holding the opponent's arm or karate gi to unbalance him even more.

Uchi: Striking Techniques

URAKEN UCHI (Backhand Strike)

1. From the hidari kamae, use your elbow like a lever.

2. The fist strikes with the back part of the hand, using the knuckles of your index and middle finger to strike the opponent. The movement is the opposite of *mawashi tsuki*; afterward, it will create a fast extension of the forearm, which is parallel to the floor. Remember that with this move, velocity is key.

KENTSUI UCHI (Hammer Fist Strike)

To strike, use the side part of your fist (closest to your pinkie); the execution technique is the same as *uraken uchi*, and in both you can follow an indistinct line of execution along a horizontal or vertical plane.

TEISHO (Base of the Palm of the Hand)

1. This is a forceful strike that works well as a block, diverting a tsuki attack from your opponent, and as an effective hit to the chin or chest.

2. Bring your arm back to your left side, closing the fist and moving your right arm toward the objective.

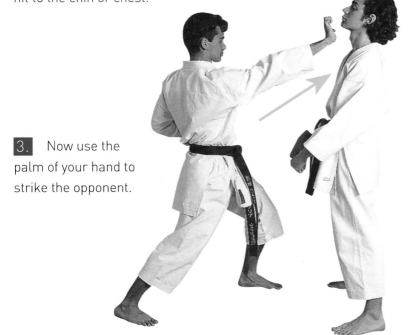

3. Now use the palm of your hand to strike the opponent.

SHUTO UCHI (Strike with the Outside of the Hand from the Inside Outward)

1. Place yourself in hidari kamae and bend your left arm in front of you at the height of the solar plexus, with the palm facing down and your right fist at your side.

2. Rotate your torso counterclockwise and elevate your elbow. Extend the forearm, making a circular motion. The palm of the left hand should be turned down when you strike.

From this same position, you can perform shuto uchi from the right to the left with both hands, but you need to change the initial position of your arm and hand, which will have the palm facing upward, and begin by placing your bent arm near your right ear. The movement can be further improved, always rotating your sides to enhance the force of impact.

NIKITE (Thrusting Hand); NIHON NIKITE (Striking Hand with One or Two Points of Main Impact)

This has the same execution principle as the previous striking technique, but it is used to strike zones that are more specific, like the eyes. Note the adopted position of the fingers in the initial and middle phases of the technique.

NUKITE (Hand Spear)

This is a striking form using the fingers: the tips of the fingers are level in order to create a unified surface impact. For example, it is used to hit the front part of the neck.

HAITO UCHI (Hand on the Back of a Knife)

This is a technique similar to Shuto Uchi, but in this case the opposite side of the hand is used for a circular strike. Remember: the thumb should be in line with the index finger and shouldn't protrude.

Elbow Strikes

YOKO EMPI (Strike with the Side of the Elbow)

Empi (elbow) can be done with different types of technical gestures to land forceful strikes on any part of the opponent's body: the face, the core, and the abdomen can all be attacked with the elbow. Empi is the name used to indicate either the part of the arm that strikes or the technique itself.

This is an effective strike when the adversary is a short distance away, and it is easily employed as self-defense. Empi can be used whether the opponent is in front, behind, or beside you.

The arm should be fully bent to create a small impact area and create the maximum striking force.

The chest and back give power to the trajectory and can be directed both up or down. Make a semicircle with the line of your arm parallel to the ground; the precise point of your elbow will depend on the direction of the strike.

1. Place yourself in *neko ashi dachi*, with the arm that will perform empi parallel to the ground; the two hands will be closed in fists.

2. Change position to *shiko dachi*, displacing the weight of your body in the direction of your opponent and striking laterally toward his solar plexus.

MAE EMPI (Frontal Strike with the Elbow)

From migi kamae, take a big step to your left, aiming to strike your opponent in the solar plexus from the front with empi.

USHIRO EMPI (Backward Elbow strike)

The opponent is behind you; situated in hidari kamae, retreat half a step with your left foot in neko ashi dachi. Rotate your hips and body toward the left strike with *ushiro empi*, reinforcing the strike with a supported push with your open right hand over your left fist.

KNEE STRIKES

Like the elbow, you can also use *hizagashira* (knee) with great force and effectiveness in short-distance combat to strike the groin, sides of the body, and ribs. People who do not possess great muscular strength can use the knee as an effective self-defense technique.

The leg should be fully bent to reduce surface impact and increase penetrative force. Extend the tips of your toes, pushing them in the opposite direction of your knee.

Use it similarly to the movement or rotation of your hips to enhance the technique's effectiveness.

Uke: Blocking Techniques

The arm also performs tsuki and uchi in order to block or laterally divert the attacks to the arms and legs.

The forearms actually perform the blocks and will, at the very least, need training and reinforcement.

The forearm is made up of different parts, and each of these parts has its own definition.

In order to block, it's necessary to be intuitive of the attack technique being fought, and then, if necessary, to perform two or more counterattacks.

All blocks can be performed in the *gyaku* (opposite) position, with the joint that stops opposite the front foot.

Depending on the area, we use different trajectories:

- Jodan attack (trajectory from below upward)
- Chudan attack (trajectory from the outside inward and vice versa)
- Gedan attack (trajectory from the top downward, sweeping to the side)

> Blocking techniques are not meant to block the trajectory of the striking attacks of the tori, but rather to divert the force of the impact, weakening it and allowing for an immediate attack.

In these examples, we show the initial phases of blocking techniques and afterward the development of the block during an attack.

Naturally, the optimal conditions for blocking an *atemi* (strike to the body) are rarely present in actual combat. In the majority of cases, there is no time to get into the described positions beforehand, which are essential for the study of different techniques; consequently, good timing and a strong visual calculation are essential.

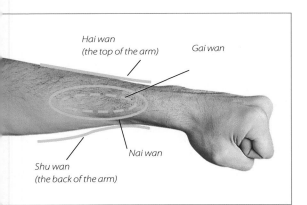

Hai wan
(the top of the arm)

Gai wan

Nai wan

Shu wan
(the back of the arm)

Accurately assess the distance of your opponent and the speed of the attack, and then apply the most adequate block to offset the atemi. If an attack produces the unexpected need to immediately come to the final block, whichever position that is, indecision can be fatal. To become confident with suitable blocks, you must train consistently.

AGE UKE (Face Block)

Age uke is used here like the *oi tsuki gedan* attack: uke lifts the arm to perform a block, intercepting and diverting the opponent's atemi; the right fist is brought back to the side.

1. From *yoi*, shown in the photo, go into Hidari Kamae, retreating with the right leg.

2. Place your left arm across your abdomen, below the right elbow, with the right arm beside your chest; tense your hands into fists. Now lift up the left forearm, almost in contact with the right. The movement of the arm is circular, wide, and on the outer part of the right arm, which withdraws. Make a cross with your forearms during the movement.

SOTO UKE (Outer Block)

From yoi (see page 105) move to hidari kamae, retreating with the right leg. Fully bend your left arm and move your fist to the right side toward your face. Extend your right arm in front of you; your torso should be turned slightly to the left, and the fists are tense.

1. Rotate your torso to the right and simultaneously direct the left forearm in a wide circular motion toward the right, bringing the right fist to your side.

2. *Soto uke* is used here against the *oi tsuki chudan* attack: uke continues the movement of the arm performing the block, intercepting and diverting the opponent's Atemi.

UCHI UKE (Inner Block)

1. From Yoi (see page 105) move into hidari kamae, retreating with the right leg. Place the left arm in front of the abdomen, below the elbow of the right arm, which should be in front of your chest; both fists are tense.

2. Move your left forearm to the left, almost touching the right as it passes. The arm movement, is wide, circular, and outward to the right arm, which withdraws and crosses the left arm.

Uchi uke is used here against the oi tsuki chudan attack: uke moves the arm in a circular motion to perform the block, intercepting and diverting the opponent's atemi. The right fist returns to your side.

SHUTO UKE (Block with the Outside of the Hand)

1. From Yoi (see page 105) move into neko ashi dachi, retreating with the right leg. The left arm is in front of your chest, over the inside of the elbow of the right arm, which is in front of your abdomen; quickly move both hands into Shuto.

2. Move the left forearm to your left side, almost touching the right arm. The movement of the arm is circular as it moves inward toward the right arm. During the movement the forearms will form a cross.

Shuto Uke is used here against the oi tsuki chudan attack: uke moves the blocking arm in a circular motion to intercept and divert the opponent's Atemi; the right hand is placed on the chest in shuto.

GEDAN BARAI (Low Sweep)

1.   From yoi (see page 105), move to hidari kamae, retreating with the right leg. Move the bent left arm close to your ear, with your right arm extended in front of your abdomen. The fists are tense.

2.   Now move the left arm down and to the left for a block, almost touching the right. The movement of the left arm will make a cross below the right arm, which is withdrawn.

Gedan barai is used here against the mae geri gedan attack: uke moves the blocking arm to intercept and divert the opponent's atemi; your right fist is at your side.

JUJI UKE (Crossed Block)

1. From yoi (see page 105) move to hidari kamae, retreating with the right leg. Lift the bent arms to your sides; the fists are tense, with the tops facing down.

2. Move the arms up 180° until the fists cross, with the left below the right.

Jujiuke is used here against the *oi tsuki jodan* attack: uke moves the two arms to intercept and divert the opponent's atemi; the hands can be closed or in the shuto position.

Kumite
(Combat)

n any martial art, combat represents the fundamental moment; because of this, karate, in many educational disciplines, would not make sense if it had no practical application.

The kumite of karate is not a fight. Even in its most open phases, it is regulated by norms that guarantee the safety of those involved (see "Controlling the Strikes" on page 25). For karatekas, it is not permitted to fight using inaccurate, poorly controlled, and confusing technical combinations. Combat exercise is always a technical exchange in which the opponents show their knowledge correctly and in a fair manner.

The practical application of techniques learned in Kihon is the kumite, the combat. In karate, your study will develop in three very different states:

- Kihon kumite (fundamental pre-established combat)
- *Ju ippon kumite* (semi-open combat)
- *Jiyu kumite* (open combat)

Kihon kumite: Preestablished fundamental combat is the direct application of the techniques that the student learns in the Kihon. The two athletes perform a singular attack and just one blocking counterattack, letting out a yell before the exercise. Generally, this type of combat occurs when the opponents are one step away from each other; a variant also exists in which the attacker repeats this three (*sanbon kumite*) or five (*gohon*

kumite) times; in this case, the counterattack is performed only after the last attack.

Ju ippon kumite: This is an intermediate level of karate. The karatekas perform the preestablished attacks and counterattacks and can choose the moment of attack.

Jiyu kumite: In open combat, the karatekas can choose the most opportune moment to attack, but they should not show the technique they intend to use. Nor is there a limitation on how many strikes can be thrown, since the attack and defense roles are open to both. In the open combat phase of the study, the instructor should make sure it does not become a fight.

KIHON KUMITE

Here we propose some of the possible attack and defense combinations that, if practiced with care and concentration, can help you enhance your skill. Uke is in yoi (see page 105) and waits for the tori's attack, which is part of hidari kamae.

1. Tori attacks in oi tsuki. Uke retreats with the right leg and performs age uke in zenkutsu dachi.

2. Now tori counterattacks in gyaku tsuki.

1. Tori attacks in oi tsuki. Uke retreats with the right leg and performs soto uke in zenkutsu dachi.

2. Now tori counterattacks in gyaku tsuki.

1. Tori attacks in oi tsuki. Uke retreats with the right leg and performs uchi uke in zenkutsu dachi.

2. Now tori counterattacks in gyaku tsuki.

1. Tori attacks in mae geri. Uke retreats with the right leg and performs gedan barai in zenkutsu dachi.

2. Now tori counterattacks in gyaku tsuki.

1. Tori attacks forward in mawashi geri. Uke retreats with the right leg and performs uchi uke in zenkutsu dachi.

2. Now tori counterattacks in gyaku tsuki.

1. Tori attacks in yoko geri. Uke retreats with the right leg and performs soto uke in zenkutsu dachi.

2. Now tori counterattacks in gyaku tsuki.

1. Tori attacks backward in mawashi geri. Uke retreats with the right leg and performs uchi uke in zenkutsu dachi.

2. Now tori counterattacks in gyaku tsuki.

1. Tori attacks in uraken uchi. Uke retreats with the right leg and performs *te uke* in zenkutsu dachi.

 2. Now tori counterattacks in gyaku tsuki.

3. Tori attacks in shuto uchi. Uke retreats with the right leg and performs uchi uke in zenkutsu dachi.

4. Now tori counterattacks in gyaku tsuki.

ADVANCED TECHNIQUE COMBINATIONS

To improve your skills, we will now show examples of some techniques in which uke is not limited to a particular counterattack but develops a diverse succession of techniques within each combination.

1. Tori attacks in oi tsuki. Uke retreats with the right leg and performs gyaku uchi uke in zenkutsu dachi.

2. Tori continues with uraken uchi.

3. Tori follows with *hiza geri*, a knee strike to the stomach.

4. Tori moves forward with the right leg, finishing with *otoshi empi*, an elbow strike to the upper back.

1.   Tori attacks in oi tsuki. Uke retreats with the right leg and performs gyaku uchi uke in zenkutsu dachi.

2.   Afterward, Uke supports tori with the right wrist and moves the supporting leg to the left. Uke continues with mawashi geri.

3. Uke rotates the hips to the right, supporting the right foot in front of tori and holding the wrist of tori's strike with *teisho*.

4. Uke finishes with uraken uchi.

1.   Tori attacks in oi tsuki. Uke retreats with the right leg and performs shuto uke in neko ashi dachi.

2.   Uke continues with *nukite hidari zenkutsu dachi.*

3.   Now, holding on to tori, uke strikes with yoko geri.

1. Tori attacks in mawashi geri. Uke retreats with the right leg and performs shuto uchi uke in zenkutsu dachi.

2. Uke holds tori's right arm and counterattacks with *mawashi empi*.

3. Uke continues with uraken uchi.

4. Uke retreats with the left leg, finishing with mae geri.

1. Tori attacks in oi tsuki. Uke retreats with the right leg and performs uchi uke in zenkutsu dachi.

2. Afterward, uke counterattacks with *kizami geri* (kick with the front leg).

3. Uke returns to zenkutsu dachi performing *haito uchi*.

4. Uke finishes with yoko geri.

1. Tori attacks in mawashi geri. Uke retreats with the right leg and performs soto uke from shiko dachi.

2. Uke rotates and retreats with the right leg toward the right until it is in neko ashi dachi. Uke counterattacks, rotating over the right side with migi uraken uchi.

3. Uke finishes with *migi ushiro geri*.

1. Tori attacks in mawashi geri. Uke retreats with the right leg and performs uchi uke in zenkutsu dachi.

2. Uke counterattacks with mawashi geri.

3. Uke finishes with gyaku mawashi tsuki.

1. Tori attacks in yoko geri. Uke retreats with the right leg and performs gedan barai in zenkutsu dachi.

2. Moving with the left foot toward the left, uke counterattacks with *fumi komi*.

3. Uke continues with yoko geri.

4. Now, with the right foot supported on the floor, uke performs a counterclockwise rotation: *ushiro mawashi geri.*

1. Tori attacks in yoko geri. Uke retreats with the right leg and performs gedan barai in zenkutsu dachi.

2. Without changing the support of the right foot, uke counterattacks with hidari mawashi geri gedan directly to tori's ribs.

3. With the left leg supported, uke attacks with *mawashi tsuki*.

4. Tori finishes by performing *ashi barai*.

1. Tori attacks in *ushiro geri*. Uke steps back with the right leg and performs *te uke* in zenkutsu dachi.

2. Uke moves the weight of the left foot and counterattacks with yoko geri.

3. Uke bends the same leg in fumi komi.

4. Uke returns to zenkutsu dachi and finishes with gyaku tsuki.

1. Tori attacks in *ushiro mawashi*. Uke anticipates the attack, stepping back with the right leg and squatting.

2. Squatting has prepared uke to perform, with a clockwise rotation, an ushiro mawashi geri directed at tori's supporting leg, transforming it into a low sweep.

3. After bringing tori to the ground, uke rises and finishes with fumi komi.

1. Tori attacks in mae geri. Uke retreats with the right leg and performs gyaku gedan barai in zenkutsu dachi.

2. Uke counterattacks with uraken uchi and controls tori by holding his right shoulder.

3. Uke performs fumi komi.

4. Uke finishes with *kakato geri*.

1. Tori attacks in mae geri. Uke retreats with the right leg and performs gedan barai in zenkutsu dachi.

2. Uke counterattacks with mae geri.

3. Uke bends the same leg in mawashi geri.

4. Now uke supports the right foot and, rotating counterclockwise, switches the supporting foot and performs Ushiro mawashi geri.

Kata
(Forms, Models)

This is an advanced-level exercise, thanks to which the karate student learns to perform all positions, diverse attack combinations, and ordinary defenses according to blocking schemes, which can sometimes be very complex.

During the execution of the kata, the karate student participates in an imaginary combat against one or more opponents who attack her from every direction; every kata has a point of stable departure that coincides perfectly with the point of an opponent's arrival.

More than one hundred kata exist, many of which differ according to style, and they preserve the original tradition from the schools of Okinawa. While it is certainly true that these kata encompass a great variety of moves and techniques, we will focus on the most fundamental kata here.

The kata is performed often; a system of training known as *bunkai* also exists, in which the karate student can realistically practice technical sequences with training partners.

The kata belongs primarily to two areas of style:

- *Shorei*
- *Shorin*

The shorei style interprets the kata as wide, fast techniques like *heian*, *bassai*, and *kanku*. Also belonging to this last section are heian and *pinan*, the kata that we will show you how to perform.

Attention: in order to show you a complete view of these technical movements, the point of view of the kata has been moved 45° from the normal point of execution.

Kata, Heian, and Pinan

The words "Heian" (Japanese) and "Pinan" (Chinese-Okinawanese) literally mean "large peace," "form of peace and tranquillity," and "peaceful mind." They indicate the basic forms of the shuri-te system, in the shorin style. In total, they are composed of five kata:

- *Pinan shodan*
- *Pinan nidan*
- *Pinan sandan*
- *Pinan yondan*
- *Pinan godan*

And:

- *Heian shodan*
- *Heian nidan*
- *Heian sandan*
- *Heian yondan*
- *Heian godan*

According to tradition, it was the Master Itosu Anko who devised the pinan forms combined with *kata kusanku*.

However, the pinan forms can also be deflected by *kata channan*.

It's said that it was the *bushi* (warrior) Matsumara Sokon,

Itosu's teacher, who developed these kata from ancient Chinese forms. On the other hand, it could have simply been an old series of Chinese Kata.

Common opinion attributes the first and second Pinan to Matsumura Sokon. But it was Master Itosu Anko who developed and taught them at the turn of the twentieth century. The founder of shotokan style, Gichin Funakoshi, changed the order of the kata, inverting the execution of the first two.

The karate styles that are shown here are: shotokan, shitoryu, wadoryu, shorinryu, and other derivatives of Master Itosu's school.

The Kiai

An important aspect of martial arts, and in this case karate, that intrigues and fascinates neophytes is, without a doubt, the *kiai*, or "union of energy." The kiai is the art of concentrating all physical and mental energy to achieve a preestablished goal.

It's a cry emitted, for example, during an attack, generally with a strong contraction of the diaphragm, which produces vibrations equal to or greater than those emitted by the opponent; thanks to this, it's possible to intimidate an opponent, allowing for an easier and more efficient victory.

The effectiveness of kiai has never been proven, but it also hasn't been disproven. Generally, the kiai allows those who perform it to eliminate negative thoughts from their spirit, which do not have the nature "of pure energy" (chi).

Furthermore, the kiai helps free, in very little time, a great mental and physical strength, whose vibrations will influence and modify the analogous vibrations of the opponent. It is also used in the *kuatsu* (resuscitation) technique by experts to revive people who are unconscious due to traumatic injuries or other causes.

In karate, the kiai is used to highlight the effectiveness of a technique during combat or in certain phases of kata. In effect, the difference between the execution of a technical combination with the kiai in its final phase and one without the "cry that kills" is easily recognized.

KATA HEIAN SHODAN

2. Yoi (prepared) takes the position of hachiji dachi.

1. Ritsurei: foot salute.

3. Gedan barai: performed descending into zenkutsu dachi to the left; the right foot rotates but does not move.

4. *Oi tsuki*: Advance from the previous position with the left foot. The weight is centered on the sole of the foot. The fist attack is chudan.

5. Change directions 180° and perform gedan barai.

6. *Kentsui uchi*: Keep the left foot firm and move the right backward until it reaches the left. Use a hammer-fist attack.

7. Oi tsuki: Move forward into oi tsuki chudan.

8. Gedan barai: The right foot does not move; the left moves forward, up, and to the right, passing the right foot. Place yourself in hidari zenkutsu dachi gedan barai.

9. Shuto age uke: Stay firm and perform a left arm block.

10. Age uke: Move forward in zenkutsu dachi and block with the right arm.

11. Age Uke: Move forward in zenkutsu dachi and block with the left arm.

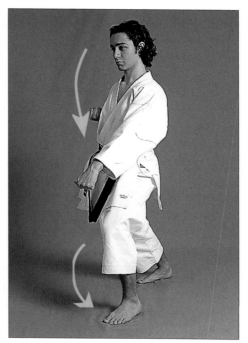

12. Age uke: Move forward in zenkutsu dachi. Block with the right arm and perform the kiai.

13. Gedan barai: Rotate 270° to the left; keeping the right foot firm, move it closer to the left. Bringing the left fist to the right ear and rotating counterclockwise, finish with Hidari gedan barai.

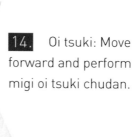

14. Oi tsuki: Move forward and perform migi oi tsuki chudan.

15. Mawatte gedan barai: Switch the position.

16. Oi tsuki: Move to the left.

17. Gedan barai: Rotate 90° counterclockwise.

18. Oi tsuki: Move to the right.

19. Oi tsuki: Move left.

20. Oi tsuki: Move right.

21. Shuto uke: Keep the right foot firm and move the left foot toward it. Rotate counterclockwise 270° and stop in hidari kokutsu dachi.

22. Shuto uke: Keep the left foot firm and stop turning at 45° to the right, always in kokutsu dachi.

23. Shuto uke: Switch the position with a block to the right in kokutsu dachi.

24. Shuto uke: Keep the right foot firm and stop rotating at 45° to the left, always in kokutsu dachi.

25. Yoi: Resume the initial position and perform hachiji dachi.

26. Ritsurei: Foot salute.

KATA PINAN SHODAN

1. Ritsurei: Foot salute.

2. *Musubi dachi*, first part: Prepare yourself for the execution of the kata.

3. Musubi dachi, second part.

4. Soto hachiji dachi.

5. *Hidar neko ashi dachi*: Perform *chudan yoko uke*.

6. Neko ashi dachi: Perform *ken uchi komi* without moving.

7. Hachiji dachi: Perform *kentsui uchi komi*.

8. Migi neko ashi dachi: Rotate 180° and perform chudan yoko uke.

9. *Ashi dachi*: Perform ken uchi komi without moving.

10. Hachiji dachi: Perform *kensui uchi komi*.

11. Chudan yoko uke: Rotate clockwise 180°.

12. Chudan yoko geri: perform without moving.

13. Hidari neko ashi dachi: Rotate 180° counterclockwise, performing shuto uke with your left arm.

14. Migi neko ashi dachi: Move forward and perform shuto uke, this time with the right arm.

15. Hidari neko ashi dachi: Move forward and repeat shuto uke with the left.

16. Migi zenkutsu dachi: Move forward and perform *shihon nukite* while using the kiai.

17. Hidari neko ashi dachi: Rotate 225° counterclockwise, performing shuto uke.

18. Migi neko ashi dachi: Move forward and perform shuto uke again, changing the arm.

19. Migi neko ashi dachi: rotate 90° clockwise and perform shuto uke again.

20. Hidari neko ashi dachi: Move forward and perform shuto uke again.

21. Zenkutsu dachi: Rotate 45° counterclockwise, performing gyaku chudan yoko uke.

22. Mae geri: Move forward.

23. Migi zenkutsu dachi: Perform chudan gyaku tsuki.

24. Migi Zenkutsu Dachi: Perform gyaku chudan yoko uke without moving.

25. Mae geri: Move forward, performing the move with the other leg.

26. Hidari zenkutsu dachi: Perform chudan gyaku tsuki.

27. Hidari zenkutsu dachi: Move forward and perform a right *chudan yoko hiji sasae uke*.

28. Hidari zenkutsu dachi gedan barai: Rotate 225° counterclockwise.

29. Migi zenkutsu dachi: Move forward and perform jodan age uke.

30. Migi zenkutsu dachi gedan barai: Rotate 90° counterclockwise.

31. Hidari zenkutsu dachi: Move forward and perform jodan age uke.

32. *Soto hachiji dachi zanshin:* Rotate the body and assume an alert position.

33. Musubi dachi, first part: Prepare for the final kata.

34. Musubi dachi, second part.

35. *Soto hachiji dachi*, final position.

36. Ritsurei: Foot salute.

Conclusion

I t can seem ambitious to try to teach all the complexities of a martial art style in a book; naturally, we consider it necessary to take classes with a teacher. The object of this book is to offer the beginner a comprehensive overview of the basic techniques of karate. This book can also act as a great technical support for students wishing to learn more about the general discipline, regardless of their chosen style of practice. The fundamental principles, moves, and techniques of karate shown here constitute the general "grammar" all of the schools.

Through the lessons of this book, we've presented an occasion to learn the first steps of the discipline. It is, of course, not enough to know the execution of the principle techniques to become a good karate student—that's why we have included the combat practices. We have also ensured a useful training model for those who do not have the opportunity to attend regular classes.

If you're encouraged by this text and decide to enroll in a class, remember to visit a few different sessions beforehand: choosing the right teacher is important. Thanks to this book, you will have the opportunity to judge if a teacher's lessons fit with your goals. Are the techniques performed correctly? Are the explanations clear? Are the lessons directed too much toward competition? These are some questions that should be asked, and the answers will influence your activity. If you wish to learn karate for the the simple pleasure of studying a martial art and keeping fit, a teacher who is too strict or too focused on competition will not be a good match for you. For the same reason, if you feel inclined toward competition, a teacher who prepares lessons oriented toward the tradition of the discipline will not be satisfactory either. Whatever your aspirations, here's one final piece of advice: practice consistently. If you do not attend classes regularly, use this book; you will derive great enjoyment from it.

Glossary

atemi   Any blow to the body, delivered with any part of the body and hitting any part of the opponent's body.

bunkai   Literally "analysis" or "disassembly"; usually, a third party watches a tori and uke perform offensive and defensive kata to analyze the movements and discover the cause and effect of each technique.

dan   Literally "grades"; a ranking system used in many Japanese martial arts, in which levels are divided by experience and marked by belt colors.

dojo   Literally "place of the way"; traditionally a place where students of Japanese martial arts went to train and study their discipline, although today the term is broad and connected to many physical training facilities in Japan.

kakato   The heel of the foot, used as the point of contact during some kicking techniques.

karate gi   The outfit worn by students of karate, consisting of a cotton, waist-length robe, ankle-length pants, and belt, the color of which depends on the athlete's experience and skill.

karatekas   Athletes who study and practice karate.

kata   One of the principle ways of learning and practicing karate, in which an athlete follows a formal system of prearranged forms and exercises.

kihon   Literally "basics," or "fundamentals"; a concept that covers all essential karate training, including form, breathing, stances, and offensive techniques.

kogeki   To attack or cut down; a word applied to the karateka performing offensive techniques during a match or training session.

koshi   The ball of the foot, used as the landing point for many kicking techniques.

kumite   Literally "grappling hands"; along with kata and kihon, one of the main sections of karate, in which a karateka trains against an opponent using techniques learned during lessons.

kyu   A way of ranking the experience level of karate students, generally indicating a lower experience and skill level than dan.

oi tsuki   Literally "lunge punch"; considered the most powerful punch in karate, as the karateka steps as he strikes, reinforcing the thrust with the forward movement of the step.

ritsurei   A standing bow performed between two karatekas before a competitive match or training session.

seiken   The knuckles of the index and middle finger when the hand is balled into a fist, used for many throws and striking techniques.

shuto   The outer edge of the hand, used as the point of contact for some throws and defensive techniques.

sokuto   The outer edge of the foot, an area used as the point of contact for some kicking techniques.

teisho   The lower part of the hand, used as the area of contact for some striking techniques.

tori   Literally "to take" and "to pick up"; the person who performs the actions during training exercises against their training partner (uke).

uke   Literally "receiving body"; the person who, during training sessions, receives the techniques performed by their training partner (tori).

yoi   A position indicating that the karateka is ready for the execution of techniques, done with the arms moved forward, fists closed, and elbows slightly bent.

zarei   Literally "seated bow"; a bow done sitting on the ground at the beginning and end of each training session to establish respect between the karateka and sensei.

Further Reading

Books

Funakoshi, Girchin. *Karate-Do: My Way of Life*. New York, NY: Kodansha USA, 2013.

Kanazawa, Hirokazu. *Karate: The Complete Kata*. New York, NY: Kodansha USA, 2013.

Martin, Ashley P. *The Shotokan Karate Bible, Second Edition: Beginner to Black Belt*. New York, NY: Bloomsbury USA, 2016.

Websites

Karate Coaching

www.karatecoaching.com

A karate resource that provides members with tips and techniques to improve a student's skills.

World Karate Federation

www.wkf.net

The official site for the World Karate Federation, which houses sport rules and regulations as well as information on international competitions.

Index